Alexander the Great

The story of the invincible Macedonian king

MARTIN HOWARD

A & C Black • London

First published 2010 by
A & C Black Publishers Ltd
36 Soho Square, London, W1D 3QY

www.acblack.com

Text copyright © 2010 Martin Howard

The right of Martin Howard to be identified as the author
of this work has been asserted by him in accordance with
the Copyrights, Designs and Patents Act 1988.

ISBN 978-1-4081-2651-6

A CIP catalogue for this book is available from the British Library.

Printed and bound in Great Britain
by CPI Cox & Wyman, Reading RG1 8EX.

Prologue
Child of the Gods

Queen Olympias stood on the palace wall, staring up at the sky where the priests said the stars made pictures of the gods. It was 356 BC, almost two and a half thousand years ago. The cool summer evening air gently stirred the golden hair of the baby in her arms. The beautiful queen glanced down into the face of her sleeping son and remembered the dream she'd had before he was born.

She had been struck by a thunderbolt, then a fire had flared in her belly; a fire that had burned with a glorious light. Soon afterwards, her husband, King Philip II of Macedonia, had had another strange dream. In the king's dream, the child she now held had been a lion.

Many people thought Queen Olympias had magical powers. Perhaps they were right, she thought, looking down at her son. She had known immediately that the dreams were messages from Zeus, the king of the gods, but to make sure, she visited the high priest at the Temple of Zeus in her homeland of Epirus.

'The son you shall have will not only be the child of you and King Philip, but the child of Zeus himself,' the old man had said as they sat together beneath an old oak tree. 'He will be no ordinary child, but a hero, as brave as a lion and as dazzling as fire. But you must keep this secret from him until he is ready to seek his destiny, for his path will be dangerous. His life will be like a fire that burns fierce and bright. But the fire that burns the brightest, never burns for long.'

That had been months ago, before her son was born. Now Queen Olympias held the tiny boy tight and looked into the night sky. It was said that the Macedonian royal family was descended from the champion Herakles, whose father was Zeus himself. Her son truly *was* the child of the gods. Carefully, Queen Olympias held the baby up to the stars, and spoke his name. The breeze would carry it away for Zeus to hear.

'Alexander,' she whispered.

1

The Boy Who Would
Be King

Alexander ran through the palace corridors. He was dirty and scratched from rolling in the dusty courtyard with his toy soldiers, fighting great battles with the little wooden army.

'Mother!' he yelled as he ran into the cool rooms she occupied. 'I heard the sound of horses. Has the king returned? Is Father home?'

Queen Olympias clutched Alexander's younger sister Cleopatra tightly and frowned at her son. 'Where have you been?' she asked sternly. 'Lanike has been looking everywhere for you. You worry us to death, running off all the time.'

Lanike was Alexander's nurse. She was always looking for him and as far as he was concerned she could carry on doing so. She wasn't happy unless he was sitting quietly and still, so he didn't mess up his clothes.

'Forget Lanike,' he cried. 'Is it true? Is the king back at Pella? May I see him?'

Alexander rarely saw his father. On the day he'd been born, King Philip had won a famous victory over the city of Potidaea, and he'd been fighting battles ever since. It seemed to Alexander that his father was always at war, but during the brief times when the king returned to Macedonia's capital city of Pella, the boy loved to sit on his knee and listen to tales about the crash and roar of battle; the clash of sword on shield, the shouts of the men, and the deadly rain of arrows. To Alexander, King Philip II of Macedonia was the greatest warrior who'd ever lived. His father had invented a completely new way of fighting, by organising his troops into large rectangles of soldiers armed with long spears. He called them *phalanxes* and on the battlefield they were all but invincible.

Queen Olympias looked down into her son's dark-blue eyes and smiled. 'Yes, your father has returned, but you cannot be presented to the king looking like that. Go find Lanike and tell her to take you to the baths.'

Two hours later, Alexander was sitting on the steps of the throne dressed in a simple white tunic and sandals with a red cloak over his shoulders. Eyes wide in awe, he looked up at King Philip. His father, however, ignored him, listening instead to reports from his generals and staff, and receiving noble visitors who had come to congratulate him on his latest victories against the hill tribes of Thrace to the north.

At last, Philip finished talking and beckoned to his son. Nervously, Alexander got to his feet and stepped towards his grim-faced father.

The king was not tall, but he was built like a warrior with a strong, powerful-looking body. Beneath his thick beard were the scars of old wounds taken in battle, and there were more scars on the king's thickly muscled arms and legs. He looked his son up and down.

'You've grown,' he said, then took the boy in his arms.

Respectfully, the other men in the throne room withdrew. When he had finished hugging the boy, amazed as always at how sweet he smelled, King Philip pushed him back.

Alexander stood as straight and tall as he could, like a guard at attention. He wanted his father to be proud of him.

'Aye, you've grown,' the grizzled old warrior said softly. 'Tell me, boy, do you know what this is?' He tapped what looked like a golden sun on the breastplate of his armour.

'It is the Argead Star, the symbol of the Macedonian king,' Alexander said. 'It has twelve points, one for each of the gods on Mount Olympus, and –'

'Yes, yes, that's enough,' Philip laughed. 'You've been learning, too, then?'

'Mother told me about it.'

For a second, a cloud appeared on the king's face, then he laughed and tousled Alexander's hair. 'Did she indeed? Well, that's good. Yes, it is the royal star of Macedonia. And one day, Alexander, when I am dead, you will wear it as King.'

Alexander stared at his father. It had never occurred to him that the king might die. 'But, sire,' he said. 'You cannot die. You're a hero, like the ones in the old stories Lanike tells me.'

Philip hunched over in his throne and looked his son in the eye, his face serious. 'Even heroes die, Alexander,' he said softly. 'And one day Macedonia will need a new king; a king who is strong and wise. You are my heir and I have been thinking about you while I was away.'

'What's an heir?' Alexander asked.

'An heir is next in line to the throne. When I am gone, you will become king. And you must be ready for that day. You are six years old now, and it's time your training began.'

Alexander grinned. 'I will learn quickly, Father,' he replied loudly. 'And next year I will fight alongside you on the battlefield.'

Philip proudly clapped a hand on his son's shoulder, then continued, 'A good king must not only learn to fight, Alexander. My goal is to make Macedonia the greatest kingdom in the world. To rule such a kingdom takes wisdom and knowledge. And *that* you will never learn on the battlefield.'

Seeing Alexander's mouth sag with disappointment, Philip waved a finger in front of the boy's face. 'Do not worry, my son, you will soon learn to be a warrior, but you must have other teachers, too.'

The king sat up and waved a hand. From the back of the hall, an old man approached the throne. He was thin and bent, walking with the aid of a stick. There was an unkind gleam in his eye.

'This is Leonidas,' said Philip. 'From this day on, he will be your teacher. You will obey him at all times and learn everything you can.'

Alexander stared in disbelief at the twisted old man. What could he possibly learn from this old crow? He started to protest, but his father clapped him on the shoulder again and said, 'Make me proud, young king.'

2
Bucephalus

The next four years passed quickly for Alexander. Leonidas was a serious teacher and a prying, strict old fool. Alexander knew that the old man checked through his clothes to make sure he didn't wear anything too luxurious. Leonidas hated soft living and liked nothing better than to keep the young prince hard at work, both in the schoolroom and outside, where Alexander was constantly made to sweat while training with sword, spear and bow.

Although he would never have admitted it, Leonidas was secretly impressed with his student. Alexander never complained and threw himself into whatever task he was given with vigour. He had a mind that soaked up everything he was taught, and he was a skilled athlete and swordsman. What Alexander liked best, though, was to study the old legends of heroes like Herakles, and his geography lessons about mighty Persia, the vast empire to the east. It was said that Persia contained wonders that few had ever seen: mountains so tall that no man could climb them, endless deserts that could not be crossed, and wealth beyond the imagination. When he heard these stories, Alexander's face would take on a strange, faraway look, and Leonidas would wonder what the boy was thinking.

The prince finished the task that Leonidas had set them and looked around the room. Boys of various ages were bent over their work. King Philip thought it was important that his child should grow up with the sons of his Macedonian nobles. After all, one day they would be Alexander's generals and palace staff.

Over the years, the students had become his friends, but none more so than the boy who sat next to him, scratching his black curls and trying to peer over Alexander's shoulder.

Stifling a laugh, Alexander covered his writing with one arm. Let Hephaestion do his own work, he thought. He'd get cross that his friend wouldn't let him copy and challenge him to a wrestling competition later. Alexander always enjoyed that.

There was to be no wrestling that day, though. As the class finished, the boys heard shouting from the direction of the palace stables. As one, they rushed there to see what the uproar was about, leaving Leonidas shouting to a classroom full of empty air.

Alexander and Hephaestion were the first to arrive and skidded to a halt in the dust. Before them stood the king, surrounded by friends. Everyone was watching four or five stable lads and Philonicus the Thessalian horse trader trying to calm a magnificent horse. It was as black as night, except for a blazing white shape like a bull's skull on its forehead. And it was furious. The horse was bucking and rearing, dragging everyone who tried to hold it down through the dirt, as if they weighed no more than flies.

Alexander felt something stir deep in his heart.

'It's a superb animal, is it not, sire?' shouted Philonicus, while desperately pulling on the rope.

The horse ignored Philonicus and reared up on

its hind legs, shaking its head. There was blood mixed with foam at its mouth and it was covered in sweat. As Alexander watched, the horse struck out with one of its front hooves, forcing Philonicus to duck and stagger back, squealing.

Philonicus looked over his shoulder at King Philip and shouted, 'He is the finest horse I have ever seen, sire, and a bargain at just thirteen talents.'

Alexander gasped. Thirteen talents was an enormous sum of money. A fortune for any man.

'You are as crazy as the horse, Philonicus,' the king laughed. 'It will kill anyone who tries to ride it.'

Alexander stepped forward. Hephaestion caught his arm and hissed, 'What are you doing?'

Shaking Hephaestion off, Alexander approached his father. 'I will ride him,' he said simply.

King Philip looked down, amazed. 'You?' he growled. 'How could a boy still in school hope to tame a beast like this? And besides,' he added with a laugh, 'where would you find thirteen talents?'

Alexander looked up at his father. 'You will buy him for me, and if I fail to tame him then I will owe you the money. If I do tame him, he will be mine as a gift.'

By now, everyone had fallen silent. Philip looked into his son's eyes and saw something there that he had never seen before. He started to say something, to stop his son going near the deadly animal. But instead he stepped back and said quietly, 'Very well.'

Alexander nodded to his father and walked out in front of the small crowd. With a wave of his hand, he made the onlookers fall back. Then he let his cloak fall to the ground and shouted for the stable boys to drop their ropes. They obeyed and rushed to safety. Alexander moved closer, slowly. The horse pawed at the ground with a front hoof, tossing its head from side to side. Under his breath, Alexander began speaking to it, quietly and calmly telling the beast that it would be his horse, that he would always look after it and that they were meant to be together.

Soon, Alexander was by the horse's head. Taking up one of the trailing ropes, he carried on whispering to it and gently began pulling the horse round so that it could no longer see anyone but him. Little by little, it became calmer. Alexander put his hand on the huge creature's cheek and came closer until their heads were together. Then, still talking, he twisted his hands in the horse's mane and pulled himself up to sit across its wide back.

The horse snorted and reared, its feet pawing at the air, but Alexander put a hand on its shoulder and it became calm again. Squeezing with his legs, the prince urged the horse into a walk and gently pulled its mane until it had turned to face the crowd again.

For a long moment nobody moved or spoke, too astonished to even breathe. Then King Philip, almost bursting with love and pride, shouted, 'My son, you must find a bigger kingdom. Macedonia is too small for you!'

Stroking his new horse's neck, Alexander called back, 'I will call him Bucephalus, the ox head, and he shall be mine for ever.'

3
Aristotle

As the years passed, King Philip's successful wars made Macedonia a strong, rich country. By 343 BC, Pella was changing quickly. Actors, artists, musicians, great teachers, engineers, merchants, and all kinds of interesting people flocked from Greece and further away to share in the country's fortune. As Alexander grew up, he and his friends learned about new ideas and styles that made the ways of Macedonia seem very old-fashioned.

At thirteen, Alexander was the perfect Macedonian prince. Handsome, generous and popular, he was a mixture of the old ways and the new. Like his ancestors, Alexander loved to hunt the wild animals around Pella and train for battle, but he also felt at home among the colourful, lively new people in the city. So much at home, in fact, that he was less than happy when King Philip told him he was to be sent away.

'I told you some years ago that a good king must be wise and clever,' said Philip patiently to his frowning son. 'You are fortunate that I can afford to buy you a gift I never had. An education with the greatest teacher alive.'

'I would rather go into battle with you, sire,' replied his son.

'There will be plenty of time for that when you are fully grown,' said Philip sternly.

'But you win so many wars that there will be nothing left for me to conquer by then,' Alexander said, still frowning. Then seeing King Philip was starting to become angry, he added, 'But I will do as you command, Father, although I don't see why I cannot continue to learn here.'

It was the king's turn to frown. Lately, his old wounds had begun to ache and he was stiffer than he used to be. He did not like to admit it, but he was getting old and it made him irritable. He was also having problems with Alexander's mother,

Olympias, who had grown more and more cold towards him with the passing years.

'For a boy your age there are too many distractions in Pella,' he said angrily. 'I have prepared a school for you where there will be nothing to take your mind off your studies. Now, go and say goodbye to your mother and sister. You leave tomorrow.'

Two days later, Alexander dismounted Bucephalus and looked around with interest. He, Hephaestion, and a few of his old school friends had been sent to a place in the woods known as Mieza. Though he was already missing the bustle of Pella, Alexander had to admit that his new home was beautiful. Paths led off between grand old trees that spread their branches, making it shady and cool, and clear streams made a pleasant babbling noise. The smell of fresh mint hung in the air.

At great expense, King Philip had ordered a schoolhouse to be built at Mieza. Leading Bucephalus toward the building, Alexander spotted a tall, skinny man wearing simple white robes by the door. He was about forty years old, with a beard and bright, small eyes. This, thought Alexander, must be the great genius, Aristotle.

As if he could read Alexander's mind, the man gave a small bow and said, 'Good afternoon, I am Aristotle. While you are here, all of you will learn to read and write in several languages. You will study the nature of the land and sea, the wind and stars.' Then he looked directly at Alexander and lowered his voice, saying, 'And I will teach *you* how to be King.'

In fact, as Alexander soon found out, Aristotle had much more than this to teach. His father had chosen well; Aristotle's immense knowledge would eventually make him almost as famous as Alexander. With his small class of pupils sat around him on a ring of stones beneath the trees, the teacher quickly showed the incredible depth of his learning. Aristotle knew everything, from new ways of bringing water to farmlands and why birds had tongues, to mathematics, medicine and history.

Alexander threw himself into his studies and Aristotle found the young prince to be the quickest and brightest of all his pupils. In turn, Alexander was deeply impressed by Aristotle, even if the teacher did tend to ramble on a bit sometimes.

He was especially impressed when Aristotle handed him a paper scroll one day, saying to him, 'Read this, it's about a warrior called Achilles. When you have finished, you can tell me what you think of it.'

The scroll contained a famous poem called *The Iliad* by the poet Homer. Alexander sat on a stone and read the first line: *Sing, O goddess, the anger of Achilles son of Peleus*. From that moment, he was hooked. For hours he barely moved, lost in the story of the great hero Achilles and his friend Patroclus. Eventually, he came to the end and, with tears in his eyes, read of Achilles' death at the hands of a worthless man called Paris.

It was a turning point in Alexander's life. 'It's amazing,' he breathlessly told Aristotle. 'When I leave here, I will become another Achilles. Hephaestion shall be like Patroclus at my side, and together we will fight and win such honour and glory that our deeds will never be forgotten.'

Aristotle stared at his pupil. If anyone else had told him the same thing, he would have laughed, but when Alexander said he was going to become a hero to equal the great Achilles, his teacher could not help but believe him.

4
Regent

The friendship between Alexander and the young men who studied alongside him grew as strong as iron over the next two years. Just as their teacher had promised, the small class learned about the natural world, about the stars and the skies, and about the world outside Macedonia.

'Persia,' Aristotle told them one day, 'is the greatest empire the world has ever known. It stretches almost to the edge of the world and only the land of India lies beyond it. Few people have ever been there and returned, but they say that in India the men have only one leg and lie on their backs to shade themselves from the sun with their massive feet. They also say that India has a great wealth of gold, which is mined by giant ants and guarded by griffins and unicorns.'

Such stories thrilled Alexander almost as much as *The Iliad*. He longed to see Persia and the mysterious land beyond it for himself.

Not all Alexander's classes were taken sitting with his friends. Now and again, Aristotle would tap him on the shoulder and lead him to a private room in the schoolhouse. There, Alexander had lessons meant only for the ears of a future king. Aristotle told him the names of those who were likely to be his enemies, and those who he could count on as friends. The prince learned of battle tactics, and how to treat a vanquished foe, and he also learned – as all kings must – that sometimes justice should be harsh.

'A king must be generous to his friends, but swift to punish those who have betrayed him,' Aristotle told him.

Alexander nodded. He had already learned as much from his father and from reading *The Iliad*.

From time to time, King Philip sent musicians and poets to entertain the class in the quiet glade of Mieza. On one occasion, a special guest arrived:

the sculptor Lysippus. He was a short, stocky, plain-looking man with big hands. When Alexander first saw him ride up, he thought that Lysippus might be any common farmer or workman. Over the following weeks, however, the sculptor proved why he was the most famous artist in all of Greece.

Alexander stared in awe at Lysippus' final work; his own head, carved from stone, with the hair curling to its neck and a young, handsome face. It was beautiful, and simple.

'It is magnificent,' whispered Aristotle. 'Look at the eyes. It is a work of genius.'

Alexander nodded. Lysippus had captured his expression perfectly. The statue's eyes seemed thoughtful, proud and hungry. It was as if Alexander was looking into the future and could not wait to start winning the glory that waited for him there.

'From this day onwards, no one but you will ever make a sculpture of me,' he declared.

The days of peaceful learning could not last forever for a young man who was heir to a throne. Alexander's schooling came to a sudden end one morning in 340 BC when King Philip rode into Mieza. Aristotle's students rushed from the schoolhouse at the sound of horses, and Alexander was amazed to find the king himself dismounting. His father, he thought, looked older than before. His hair had more grey in it, and he walked with a limp.

Philip, in turn, gazed at his son. Although Alexander would never be the tallest of men, he was now sixteen and his skin glowed with health from the exercise and simple life he was leading. The sun had given his hair golden streaks like a lion's mane. King Philip felt a rush of pride in his son and remembered the dream he'd had that Alexander would one day become a lion.

The prince stepped forward with excitement in his eyes. 'What news, Father?'

Philip clapped his son on the shoulder. 'Your schooldays are over, my son,' he said. 'Macedonia needs you. I am taking the army to war.'

Alexander's eyes widened. 'And will you take me with you?' he demanded.

Philip laughed at his son's fierce expression and his hunger to prove himself in battle. 'Not this time, Alexander,' he said. 'I have a different task in mind. I want you to sit upon the throne of Macedonia and rule my country as Regent while I am gone.'

5

Into Battle

Alexander was overjoyed to see his mother and Cleopatra again, and surprised to see his sister had grown from the child he had left behind into a beautiful young woman. But there was little time to talk to either of them. The city was bustling to get ready for Philip's march to Byzantium in the east, and the king made sure that Alexander spent every hour of the day learning how to rule the country while he was away at war.

A few days after returning from Mieza, Philip gave his son new armour and presented him to the army. With Bucephalus snorting beneath him and the breeze catching the white plume of his helmet, Alexander watched as phalanx after phalanx of soldiers raised their spears to him and cried his name. Then the cavalry came riding past. The drumming hooves of thousands of horses made the earth shake and raised great clouds of dust. When the riders began banging their spears against their shields to greet Alexander, it sounded like thunder. Again and again, his name was shouted to the heavens.

'From this day forward, you will command the cavalry,' Philip told him. 'And these will be your troop leaders.' He gave a signal and a number of horses cantered forward from the great mass of men. Alexander couldn't stop himself grinning. The troop commanders were his old school friends, with Hephaestion in front.

'Hail, Ptolemy! Hail, Leonnatus! Hail, Seleucus, Perdiccas, Lysimachus, Craterus and Hephaestion!' Alexander cried, laughing and saluting the men with his own spear.

In reply, his friends beat their shields with all their might.

The feast that Alexander had that night was wild, but as the months passed, his excitement at being in charge of the kingdom faded.

'To think I dreamed of becoming as great as Achilles,' he complained to Hephaestion. 'All I do is sit on my father's throne, hearing reports and signing papers.'

'Don't worry,' replied Hephaestion, putting an arm around his friend's shoulder. 'We'll get our chance one day, and when we do, we'll show the world a fight it will never forget.'

'I hope you're right, Hephaestion. Otherwise I'll go down in history as Alexander the Penpusher.'

The conquests that Alexander dreamed of seemed very far away. He was now seventeen and eager to make a name for himself in battle. But instead, an endless stream of people swarmed around him. Messengers from his father in the east gave him daily reports of the army's progress, and expected to return with Alexander's own reports, while advisers and nobles queued to see him and squabble with each other over every tiny detail of running the kingdom. Meanwhile, spies and messengers arrived from every corner of Greece and the lands that Philip had conquered, bringing news that trouble was brewing. With Philip away, the tribes to the north were restless, while in the

Greek city of Athens to the south, a man called Demosthenes was stirring up trouble against Macedonia.

'It is in the palace that you will learn to be a king,' Philip had told his son before leaving for Byzantium. 'To rule a country, you must make important decisions every day, listen to every piece of news, and be ready to act in an instant.'

So when a tribe called the Maedi in the northern land of Thrace suddenly rebelled, Alexander remembered his father's advice. Thrace was a big country made up of a patchwork of small kingdoms. It was Philip's proudest boast that he had conquered all of them, but Alexander knew that if one small part of Thrace overthrew Macedonian rule, it might easily start more rebellions. He could not allow that to happen, and so he led a small army to the lands of the Maedi at a gallop.

Alexander's victory was quick and complete. The Maedi tribesmen were badly organised fighters, while Alexander's troops were highly trained. The prince soon proved himself a cool and deadly commander, as well as a fierce warrior. When the fighting was over, Alexander showed he had learned the lessons of Aristotle and his father well. Beating the Maedi in battle was not punishment enough for their treachery. He remembered that a king must be generous to his friends but harsh to his enemies.

'Every Maedi man, woman and child will leave these lands on pain of death,' he declared. 'They will be scattered to the winds to live wherever they can and never again rise up against Macedonia!'

To make sure the Maedi never returned, the prince ordered a new city to be built. It would be peopled with Greeks and Macedonians and named Alexandropolis. The Maedi had lost their home for ever.

6

Escape to Epirus

If Alexander had had to wait seventeen years for his first taste of battle, he did not have long to wait for his second. After his victory over the Maedi, King Philip returned from his successful campaign in Byzantium and from then on father and son fought together against the rebellious tribesmen to the north and the Greek cities to the south. Philip himself stood among the foot soldiers, while Alexander led the charging cavalry on Bucephalus. In battle after battle, they beat every enemy who dared to come against them.

In 338 BC, their latest war had been against the Greek cities in the south. Although Philip did not want to conquer Greece, many people – including

Demosthenes – thought that the powerful army of Macedonia was a dangerous threat to the free Greek cities. Demosthenes had eventually succeeded in stirring the Greek armies against Macedonia, and Alexander and his father were forced to march against them.

The Greeks were crushed, and the victorious Macedonians returned to Pella. Soon after, Alexander was summoned to his mother's rooms late one night. He hurried to the part of the palace where his mother lived, and found Queen Olympias waiting for him impatiently.

'What is it, Mother?' he asked.

The queen waved away her slaves until only the two of them sat in the light of a flickering lamp. 'Your father has fallen in love again,' she replied coldly.

Alexander shrugged. Over the years his mother and father had grown to hate one another and, as was expected of a Macedonian king, Philip had married four other wives.

'He does that all the time,' said Alexander carelessly. 'It won't last long. It never does.'

'This time it's different,' whispered Olympias.

'The girl is Eurydice. She is very beautiful and comes from a noble Macedonian family, while I am just a foreigner. She is also going to have a baby. If it is a boy, you may find that you are no longer Philip's heir.'

'This is nonsense, Mother,' scoffed Alexander. 'Look at all my father's done to prepare me to become King of Macedonia, and all the battles we've fought together.'

Olympias looked at her son in the dim light, then said slowly, 'Your father is growing old and old men do stupid things when a pretty young girl has caught their heart. You must keep your eyes and ears open.'

Although Alexander took care not show it, his mother's warning remained on his mind as the weeks passed and plans for his father's latest wedding were made. He watched the king carefully and saw – as his mother had told him – that Philip was hopelessly in love with pretty young Eurydice and did everything in his power to please her. Queen Olympias, meanwhile, was ignored.

Finally, the day of Philip and Eurydice's marriage arrived. As heir to the throne, Alexander was invited to sit close to his father at the wedding feast, while Queen Olympias was given a seat with Philip's other wives, as far away from the king as possible. Alexander did his best to control his temper as he looked from his mother, who sat silently at the far end of the hall, to the girl at his father's side, dripping in jewels that Philip had given her.

All the guests, except Olympias and Alexander, drank cup after cup of wine and the hall was soon filled with drunken laughter and the songs of musicians. Every so often, one of the wedding party would stand and toast the newlyweds, and more wine was brought. Eventually, Attalus, Eurydice's father, rose to his feet unsteadily and lifted his cup.

'Let us drink to the royal couple,' he shouted. 'And the baby to come. May the gods give them a true heir to the throne of Macedonia.'

It was a terrible insult. At once the hall fell silent. Olympias stood, horror on her face. Every pair of eyes in the room turned to Alexander.

The prince jumped to his feet, snarling with fury and his sword in hand. 'You filthy dog,' he spat at Attalus. '*I* am the true heir to the throne. Apologise now, or I'll kill you where you stand.'

With a howl of rage, King Philip staggered to his feet, pulling his own sword from its scabbard. 'How dare you threaten the father of my bride,' he screamed and jumped at Alexander, then tripped and fell face down into the plates and cups, where he rolled drunkenly, unable to get up.

'You're too drunk to fight and too stupid to see that you've been made a fool of by a young girl,' Alexander sneered, then he turned and left, beckoning Olympias to join him.

Philip managed to get to his knees, shouting, 'I'll kill you,' as Alexander and his mother walked through the shocked guests to the door. 'No one pulls a sword on me and lives.' Then he collapsed on the floor again, drunk.

'Quickly,' said Alexander to his mother once they were some distance from the feasting hall. 'We must get away from here at once.'

Mother and son ran to the stables where Alexander swiftly readied Bucephalus and a horse for Olympias.

'We'll go to my brother, the King of Epirus,' said the queen breathlessly as she mounted. 'He will protect us.'

'Wait,' said a familiar voice from the door. 'Don't go without me.'

'Hephaestion,' Alexander said gently. 'You saw what happened. The king promised to kill me. If you come with us, your life will be in danger, too.'

Hephaestion grinned. 'But if I stay, I'll miss the adventure,' he replied.

7
The Revenge of Queen Olympias

King Philip's fury with his son lasted almost a year. Once he had sobered up, he no longer had any intention of killing Alexander, but he was still angry. Messenger after messenger was sent to Alexander in Epirus demanding he return and apologise in public.

When Alexander refused, Philip's rage turned on the King of Epirus. To avoid starting a war, Alexander and Hephaestion fled again, this time into the hills and mountains of Thrace.

In Macedonia, Eurydice gave birth to a daughter, called Europe, in 338 BC, and was soon expecting another baby. King Philip, meanwhile, began planning the boldest campaign of his life

– the invasion of Persia. With his young bride and new family, as well as the excitement of the war to come, Philip should have been happy, but he could not stop thinking about his son. Every day, he tried to push Alexander to the back of his mind, and every day, he failed. Despite what Olympias thought, Philip loved his son deeply and, as time passed, he missed him more and more. To make matters worse, Philip had exchanged harsh words with the King of Epirus, who had always been a good friend, and now there was the threat of war between the neighbouring countries. Something had to be done to set matters right and, eventually, King Philip formed a plan.

'You will marry the King of Epirus,' he told his daughter Cleopatra. 'A wedding will mend the quarrel between Macedonia and Epirus, and your brother will have to return for such a joyous occasion.'

The princess nodded. She had always known that one day Philip would choose a husband for her and though King Alexander of Epirus was her uncle, he was a young, handsome man. Cleopatra liked him.

'If it helps bring my brother back, I shall be glad to marry whomever you please, sire,' she smiled. 'But I have a question.'

'What is it, girl?'

'Will my mother be invited to the wedding, too?'

Philip scowled. His hatred of Queen Olympias had grown stronger since she had fled Macedonia with Alexander. However, for the sake of peace within his family and the kingdom, he managed to keep his temper and, through gritted teeth, told his daughter, 'Olympias is both your mother and the sister of the bridegroom, of course she will be invited.'

A carefully worded message reached Alexander in Thrace a few weeks later. The letter from Philip said that if Alexander returned for the wedding celebrations, the king was ready to forgive him. It was not the apology that Alexander had wanted, but the prince missed his father as much as his father missed him, and he was sensible enough to know that a king could never say sorry. It was enough to make Alexander race back to Pella.

A few months later, the day of the wedding between Princess Cleopatra of Macedonia and

Alexander of Epirus arrived. Thousands flocked to the palace in the Macedonian capital of Aegae to watch. King Philip had spent a fortune. A new theatre had been built, games were planned and the finest Greek actors had arrived to entertain the wedding guests. Ambassadors and nobles had come from every corner of Philip's lands to witness the great spectacle. Beneath blue skies, it seemed that the whole world had arrived to join the celebrations.

At the palace gate, Alexander looked over his left shoulder. As was proper for the king and the heir to the throne, King Philip was standing behind him. To Alexander's left was Alexander of Epirus, the bridegroom. Alexander nodded to his uncle and flashed a quick smile of encouragement – the King of Epirus was shaking with nerves. Then the procession began to march forwards past crowds of cheering people. Alexander set his face in a look of calm dignity.

To the beat of a drum, the priests marched at the front, carrying statues of the gods. Behind them walked Alexander, his father and his uncle surrounded by bodyguards. Musicians and dancers trailing ribbons came next. The crowds clapped and yelled as the procession made its way to the theatre, where Cleopatra waited and the wedding would take place.

As the royal party walked beneath an archway that led into the theatre, the bodyguards marched away, and a deafening roar of delight went up from the people inside as they saw the king's party arriving. From the corner of his eye, Alexander caught a flicker of movement. One of the bodyguards had turned around. Probably to get a better view, Alexander thought. He turned his head to the front again and didn't see the bodyguard pull out a long dagger. Neither did he see the man run back towards King Philip. Alexander only knew that something was wrong when he heard his father grunt in shock and the crowd gasp. He turned to see the bodyguard clutching his father around the neck. Blood was dripping from King Philip's side.

As the king fell forward onto his face, Alexander pointed at the bodyguard, who was already running, and screamed, 'Get that man. Take him alive!' Then Alexander was on his knees beside his father.

King Philip was already dead. Alexander looked down into the pale face, tears streaming down his cheeks. For a few moments, he thought he would never be able to move again, but the crowd pressed in from all sides and reminded him that there might still be danger close by.

'Guards!' he shouted. 'To my sister. Close every door.'

Seeing his uncle return from chasing the murderer, Alexander looked questioningly at the King of Epirus, who shook his head.

'The guards killed the murderer,' he said. 'We'll get no answers from him now.'

Alexander would never find out why his father had been murdered, or who else had been involved in the plot to kill him. Within hours, he was galloping back to Pella. Behind him, the body of the man who had stabbed King Philip II of Macedonia had been hung up for the birds to peck.

When night fell, a dark figure came to visit the body. Queen Olympias bowed to the dead man who had killed King Philip at her command. Now it was certain that Alexander would be king and not the child Eurydice had just given birth to.

As she walked away, the queen made plans to have Eurydice's baby son killed, too. Just to be sure.

8

King Alexander

Once again, the Macedonian army was shouting Alexander's name, but now he was their king. He sat astride Bucephalus, a grim look on his face.

In the days and weeks after Philip's murder, Alexander had had to rule Macedonia harshly. Eurydice's father had been killed to stop him starting a war, and everywhere there were new dangers. With King Philip gone, the conquered lands of Thrace thought that they could win their freedom against a young man who was new to the throne. In Greece, Demosthenes was making trouble again. He, too, was convinced that Alexander was just a boy who would not be able to defend his new kingdom.

Alexander looked out over tens of thousands of trained Macedonian warriors and decided that the most dangerous of his enemies were the Greek cities to the south. Demosthenes was doing everything in his power to make them rise up against Macedonia.

'Tomorrow, we march south!' he called to his troops, and a great cheer went up in response.

Getting to Greece would not be easy though. The road from Macedonia to Greek lands lay through a valley called the Vale of Tempe in the region of Thessaly. Knowing that war with Macedonia was in the air, the Thessalians had blocked the whole valley with heavy fortifications. It was impossible for an army to climb through the mountains to either side of the valley and, if Alexander's troops tried to march through the Vale of Tempe, they would be destroyed.

The Thessalians had not planned for Alexander's cunning though. The young king studied his maps before jabbing his finger at Mount Ossa on the border of the region. Then he gave his orders.

'Bring as many miners that can be found,' he told his generals.

For the next seven days, five hundred Macedonian miners chipped away at Mount Ossa, making a stairway up its rocky side wide enough for an army to climb. On the seventh night, Alexander's troops walked up the mountain and, as the sun rose, the commander of the Thessalian army received a message from Alexander. With his jaw dropping and his face white, he heard that the Macedonian army were in Thessaly.

'But how did you get here?' he asked with clenched fists. 'It's impossible.'

The messenger looked him in the eye. 'We cut a ladder over Mount Ossa,' he said coolly. 'Nothing stops Alexander. Not even a mountain.'

The commander was faced with the choice of fighting or allowing the Macedonian army to pass. Knowing that his men alone could never win against the Macedonians, he told the messenger that Alexander could go wherever he wanted.

To the beat of a massive drum, Alexander marched his army south to the city of Corinth in a show of strength. Any ideas that Demosthenes and the Greek cities might have had that he was a weak young king were crushed as the battle-scarred Macedonians crashed through the country with Alexander, wearing his father's armour, at their head.

At Corinth, the overawed Greek leaders quickly backed down and voted to give Alexander command over all the Greek armies like his father before him. Now that he had shown his strength, Alexander decided that he should be generous, and reveal his great plan. The time had come to fulfil the dreams he had had since he was a boy. When the flames of rebellion had been stamped out in Thrace, he could safely lead his army to the east.

'The Greek cities will remain free,' he told the council at Corinth. There were nods of approval from the men around the chamber, then, with a deep breath, Alexander continued. 'But I will need as many men as Greece can spare for my army.'

Alexander looked at the faces staring at him. 'Yes,' he said, 'we will soon be ready to march on Persia. And the Great King will tremble when he hears us coming.'

As winter turned to spring in 335 BC, Alexander turned his attention to the rebellious north, leading his army into Thrace, where he cut his way through the tribes who dared to defy Macedonian rule. By now, his men, from the lowest soldier to the highest general, were beginning to realise what a dazzling leader they had in Alexander. Raised by a father whose own skills on the battlefield were legendary, and following the example of Achilles, Alexander fought like a lion. Not once did he hang back and allow his men to fight in his place. Every time the Macedonians fell upon an enemy tribe, the new king was at the front, urging his men on and battling with sword, axe and dagger. And when the fighting was over, Alexander was always to be found with the wounded, giving words of thanks to those who weren't badly hurt, and using all the medical skills he had learned from Aristotle to help the men who were.

No leader had ever shared so much of his men's danger, or cared for them so greatly. With every battle, the Macedonian army grew to love their king more and more.

Throughout the spring, Alexander and his men made their way through the northern lands, making alliances with friendly tribes, and fighting those who refused to declare him their rightful king.

After one battle, a rumour began that Alexander had been killed. Although he wasn't hurt, it spread like fire into Greece where, once again, Demosthenes thought the time had come to rid his country of the Macedonians. With Demosthenes promising money and weapons from Persia and guaranteeing that Alexander was dead, the city of Thebes declared war on Macedonia.

It took Alexander just thirteen days to bring his army from the far north to Thebes in the south. Seeing the Macedonian king alive and marching a great army before their city walls, the leaders of Thebes realised they had made a terrible mistake, but though Alexander gave them every chance he could to surrender, still they refused to make amends or back down. Instead, Thebes sent out an army through the city gates.

The battle was the bloodiest Alexander had experienced to date. The Thebans were valiant men who fought with no fear. For hour after hour under the hot Greek sun, Thebans and Macedonians battled back and forth. It seemed like the contest would continue until only one man remained standing, but then some of Alexander's troops broke into the city and freed the Macedonians who had been imprisoned there. The released men grabbed weapons and raced out of the gates to help their leader.

Caught between Macedonians both behind and in front, the Thebans had no choice but to run back inside, but still they refused to surrender. Women and children screamed as Alexander's men ran through the streets of the city, chasing down the last of the Theban warriors.

As dust settled on the battlefield, Alexander boiled with anger. He had no wish to fight the Greeks and it was a senseless waste of good men. Even so, he could not forgive Thebes. An example must be made of it to show the other Greek cities that his fury was terrible. Like the Maedi, the Thebans, too, would lose their home for ever.

'Raze the city to the ground,' he ordered with a heavy heart. 'Nothing must remain. Not a single house.'

At Alexander's word, the ancient city was destroyed so completely it was as if Thebes had never existed.

9

War on Persia

Alexander leapt over the bow of the ship he had used to sail across the Hellespont, a narrow strip of water that separated his own lands from Persia. As he waded through the warm blue sea that glittered under the sun, he threw his spear into the sand, a symbol that he would be victorious in the new land. Behind him, a cheer went up from the men still on board the fleet of ships.

He looked around at the quiet beach. From here, he would blow through Persia like a lightning storm. Alexander was certain that Persia would fall to him, especially since the last conversation he'd had with Queen Olympias before he left. In one of their private meetings in the queen's rooms, his mother had, at last, told her son the secret she had kept all his life.

'Before you were born, your father and I both had strange dreams,' she had whispered. 'The high priest agreed that they were messages sent by Zeus himself.'

A frown creased Alexander's forehead. 'What else did the high priest say, Mother?'

Queen Olympias felt a fierce pride in her son. 'He said that you were born of two fathers: Philip and Zeus, king of the gods.'

Alexander had trembled with excitement. 'If I really am the son of Zeus,' he said, his eyes glowing in the candlelight. 'Then nothing can stop me.'

'You are right,' replied Olympias. 'The high priest foretold that you would rule the world and that your life would burn like a fire, fierce and glorious.'

'Yes,' said Alexander quietly. 'I have always dreamed of glory.'

'But you must be careful,' whispered his mother with tears in her eyes. She laid a hand on his cheek. 'The fire that burns brightest never burns for long.'

That had been weeks ago and, though Alexander did not know it, it was the last time he would ever see his mother. Now, in 334 BC, at the age of 22, Alexander was standing on Persian ground. He didn't care about Olympias' fears for his life, only that he might be the son of Zeus, like Herakles before him. Soon, he would prove it in battle, but first Alexander wanted to take a short trip. Not far from where his troops were splashing ashore were the remains of Troy, where Achilles had fought and died. Before Alexander began his conquest of Persia, he wanted to see for himself the tomb of his hero.

The famous old city of Troy had fallen on hard times since Achilles' day and now it was little more than a dusty village. Nevertheless, it still held the remains of its glorious past. The people of Troy were so impressed by the handsome and noble Macedonian king that they gave him a suit of armour thought to have been worn by Achilles himself hundreds of years before. Alexander visited Achilles' tomb while Hephaestion went to the tomb of Achilles' friend, Patroclus. Then the whole army gave thanks to the gods and asked for success in their coming battles.

With the gods' blessings assured, and dressed

in Achilles' own armour, Alexander was ready. He passed orders to his generals and the army made ready to leave. With Alexander at their head, 44,000 foot soldiers and 6,000 cavalry, made up of troops from Macedonia, Greece and the tribes of Thrace, moved into Persia.

For three weeks they marched without being stopped. But ahead were 35,000 Persian troops at a place called Zeleia. It was Alexander's first obstacle in the vast country that no one thought possible to conquer.

The enemy army had found an excellent position on the high banks of the River Granicus. Alexander's army would be forced to cross the river to attack and while horses and men floundered in the water, they would be at the Persians' mercy. As Alexander approached, he saw at once that he would, again, have to be cunning to win this contest.

Turning to General Parmenion, who had been King Philip's trusted friend and who had seen more battles than any man in the army, Alexander said, 'We should wait until night falls and surprise them at dawn.'

The white-haired old soldier nodded his

agreement and the order was passed for the men to make camp, eat and rest.

As the sun sank, the Persian army drew back from the riverbank to its own camp. Alexander waited for the deepest part of the night, then quietly gave his orders. Men and horses waded across the river beneath the stars and fell into battle formation on the opposite side. Alexander breathed a sigh of relief that they hadn't been spotted. Then he signalled, and the whole army moved forward.

As dawn broke, the Persians awoke to find their camp under attack. Too late, they strapped on their armour and threw themselves onto their horses; they were already doomed. Few escaped the swords of Alexander's army, and those who did manage to get away, ran for their lives, spreading news that Alexander was coming.

As his men celebrated their victory, Alexander, as usual, was with the injured, listening to their tales of the battle and helping to patch their wounds. It was here that a messenger found him and told the king that twenty-five of his cavalry had died in the battle. Once again, Alexander showed how generous he could be to those he counted as friends. He ordered that the families of the men who had died would never want for money again, and that the sculptor Lysippus would make each man immortal by carving his image in stone. The twenty-five sculptures would be displayed in Macedonia for ever.

10
The Battle of Issus

In the ancient and vast capital city of Susa, the Great King of Persia, Darius III, fretted over Alexander's advance for almost a year before he began to gather his forces. His advisers and the chief of his army told him to let Alexander advance so deep into Persian lands that his army would be unable to escape back to Macedonia. When Alexander was far from home and help, they said, all the food for miles around would be burned and Alexander's army could be attacked when it was starving to death.

It had seemed an excellent plan but, over the months, Darius had grown ever more angry as messenger after messenger arrived with tales of the cities that had fallen to Alexander. Sardis, Ephesus, Patara and Santhus along the coast were now under Macedonian rule, and only the city of Halicarnassus was still Persian, though it was surrounded by Macedonian troops.

Now Alexander had turned inland, taking even more cities. Darius could bear it no longer.

'Gather me an army,' he had roared from the throne. 'I shall lead it myself, and show this Alexander the true might of Persia!'

From Susa, Darius travelled west to Babylon, where he watched as tens of thousands of men arrived – archers, horsemen and foot soldiers from all over the Persian Empire. When Darius' army numbered 400,000, the Great King ordered them to march.

The procession could not have been more different to Alexander's army. The Macedonian king slept each night in a simple tent and walked or rode alongside his men, sharing their hardships every day. Darius, however, travelled in a chariot made of gold, his crown glinting in the sunlight and the gold embroidered robe of the Great King flowing from his shoulders. Behind him was a long baggage train carrying all the things he might wish for. His wife, children and mother, as well as hundreds of cooks, musicians and dancers. Each night, Darius' vast tent was furnished like a palace with gold ornaments and plates, a bath the size of a small swimming pool, and an enormous bed of carved wood and gold.

After weeks of marching, in November of the year 333 BC, Darius and his army arrived at a town on the Mediterranean coast called Issus, and discovered that Alexander had passed through with his army only the day before. This was excellent news. Darius' army had come by a road through the hills while Alexander had taken the coast road. Unknown to either of the kings, the two armies had passed each other. Darius laughed in delight as his generals told him what had happened. It meant that he could now follow Alexander and surprise him from behind. Victory was assured.

Not expecting the Great King to suddenly arrive there, Alexander had left his sick and wounded men at Issus to heal. When Darius discovered the Macedonians, his delight increased even more. At last, he could begin to take revenge on his rival.

'Cut off their hands,' he ordered. 'Never again will they lift a sword or spear against a Persian.'

It was a shockingly cruel punishment but, as the screams of their comrades echoed across the town, a few Macedonians escaped. When they arrived at Alexander's camp late that night, their leader was furious to learn about Darius' treatment of his men and horrified that the Persian army was now threatening from behind. Quickly, he ordered his men to line up, and explained that they were in a very dangerous position.

'We have only one choice,' he told them. 'I know you are tired and need rest, but we must go back and prepare a surprise of our own.'

The men groaned, but their love and respect for Alexander was so strong that they would do anything for him. Wearily, they made themselves ready to march.

The next day, Darius stood and stared at the army before him.

'It's impossible,' he choked. 'They could not have got back here that quickly.' Like the Thessalians, he was beginning to learn that the impossible could not stop Alexander.

In the dark, the Macedonian king had marched back along the road, walking every step of the way alongside his troops. As his tired legs carried him onwards, Alexander had called out to the men in his army by name, reminding them of their brave deeds and how proud he was of them. With a clap on the back here and a smile there, Alexander had given them the courage they needed to carry on.

Once the Macedonian army had reached a suitable battlefield, Alexander had arranged his foot soldiers so they stood in a line eight-men deep across the narrow strip of land, with the horses of the cavalry snorting and impatiently pawing at the ground behind. To Alexander's right were tree-covered hills, to his left the sea. In front was the Persian army. In the year since he had crossed the Hellespont, Alexander had lost some men, and had left others in cities along the way. Now, he had an army of just 25,000, waiting to do battle with 400,000 Persians.

After taking the advice of his leaders, Darius gave his orders. The main Persian army was to wait behind a river, which could be easily defended, while soldiers slipped through the wooded hills to attack Alexander's men from behind. Despite the shock of finding an army waiting for him, Darius was not worried. He could not believe that such a small force could be a threat to his mighty army.

The battle began to go wrong for the Great King from the moment it started. Seeing Persians among the trees, Alexander ordered his archers into the woods. Soon the air was alive with the *vip, vip, vip* of arrows and the shouts and screams of retreating Persians.

Alexander smiled grimly. His men were outnumbered, but he knew they were the finest fighters the world had ever seen. As his archers drew back from the woods, he called to his school friends, who commanded the cavalry. With a rumble of hooves, Alexander led the horsemen forward.

The Macedonian horses crossed the river in a furious charge, and fell upon the Persians like lions. Arrows and spears rained down from the sky, but nothing could stop Alexander's cavalry. Screaming the old Macedonian war cry, 'Alalalalalai', they charged down Persian archers, and caused such a panic among the Persians' own cavalry that the enemy horses bolted from the battlefield.

Meanwhile, the long spears of Alexander's foot soldiers were beginning to falter as the great weight of Persian soldiers pressed down upon them. They fought on bravely and then, at the end of the line, close to the sea, another cavalry charge suddenly leapt past the line of battling men to close upon the Persians from the opposite side to Alexander.

Darius could not believe what he was seeing. All around him, his mighty army was being smashed to pieces by the tiny Macedonian force. Even as he watched, Alexander's men were coming closer on every side in a terrifying whirl of swords and axes. Darius looked up and, for a second, his eyes locked with those of a young man with streaks of gold in his hair riding down on him, sword lifted high.

Alexander snarled at the Great King, who had ordered the hands to be cut off sick men, and urged Bucephalus forward.

In panic, Darius turned and fled. With the Macedonian king in pursuit, he ran for his life, abandoning his golden chariot and fabulous robe, as well as his family and his riches. Seeing the Great King flee, the Persian army did the same.

The mighty Persian army had been broken. Although the Great King had escaped, it was a stunning victory for Alexander. After they had given up chasing Darius and were returning to join the rest of the army, a soldier turned to his king.

'What will you do now, Alexander?' he asked.

'Wash away the blood and sweat in the Great King's own bath,' Alexander laughed.

When he entered the Great King's captured tent, Alexander's smile disappeared. He looked around in astonishment at the rich furnishings, the jewels and the gold glinting under the light of many lamps.

'This, it would seem, is to be a king,' he said quietly. And with that, Alexander turned and went to see to his wounded men, and to award gifts to those who had been most brave.

11
The God-king

After the Battle of Issus, Alexander turned his army south and marched towards Egypt. Before giving chase to Darius, he first wanted to finish the task of conquering Persia's seaports and then move on to Egypt. The ancient and mysterious land had been under Persian rule for 200 years and it was a rich country. Alexander knew it would be a terrible shock to Darius if Egypt fell to him.

It took over a year to get there. Six Persian cities stood in his way and all had to be beaten. The first four opened their gates to Alexander easily, but the two southernmost cities, Tyre and Gaza, refused to let him in and Alexander was forced to lay siege. It was seven long months before the Macedonian army crashed through the walls of Tyre in 332 BC and another two before Gaza fell. Alexander punished the people of both cities terribly for daring to defy him. Large parts of both places were reduced to rubble, thousands of men killed, and their women and children sold into slavery.

While the Macedonian army moved south, taking city after city from Darius' empire, the Great King himself began raising more troops.

'This time there will be no mistakes,' he told his commanders. 'It will be the greatest army the world has ever seen and we will choose the battleground to suit us. When Alexander comes again, we will finish him.'

The Persians in Egypt were less willing to fight. After conquering Gaza, Alexander's army moved south without a single battle, and marched to the Egyptian capital of Memphis through cheering crowds that scattered flower petals before him. The Egyptians hated the Persians and thought that Alexander had been sent by the gods to free them from Persian rule. At Memphis, Alexander was crowned pharaoh of Egypt and worshipped as both a god and a king.

In Egypt, Alexander also learned of a place deep in the desert called Siwah, where the mysterious god Ammon dwelled. It was said that the god's oracle spoke to a favoured few and had the power to answer any question.

'I must see this oracle,' Alexander told Hephaestion one night. 'They worship me as a god here in Egypt, and my mother told me that I was the son of Zeus. I must know if it is true.'

'It's a dangerous journey,' replied Hephaestion, shaking his head.

Alexander rested a hand on his friend's arm and looked into his eyes. 'But I must know,' he said.

Hephaestion nodded. 'And, as always, I will follow you anywhere.'

Alexander took a small troop of men and his closest friends and set off for distant Siwah to the west the next day. At first, the journey was easy. Alexander and his men took the coast road, stopping at a large bay on the way. As the king looked out across the lush landscape and the sparkling sea, a thought struck him. 'This would make an excellent place for a city,' he said. 'Bring some engineers and builders.'

In time, a city was built, exactly to Alexander's plan. Named Alexandria, it would eventually become the most famous and beautiful city in the world.

Soon, the journey became more difficult. For weeks, Alexander and his men walked across the desert and were lost for days before two magical crows led them back to the right path. Eventually, they arrived, tired and dusty, at the shrine of Siwah, where the people dressed in bright colours and performed strange rituals to Ammon.

Now Alexander was to find out if he truly was the son of a god. The priest beside him, who had feathers in his hair, nodded and Alexander walked into a dark room cut into the cliff face, leaving behind the procession that had followed him.

Hephaestion was waiting as his friend came out of the room some time later. Alexander's eyes were shining.

'What did the god tell you? Hephaestion demanded.

Alexander just smiled. 'That, I shall never tell,' he whispered. 'But we should make the army ready to march again. Darius is waiting for us.'

71

12
Gaugamela

'By Zeus, I've never seen anything like it,' choked Parmenion.

'There must be a million men,' gasped Hephaestion. 'And what are those huge beasts?'

'You should have listened to Aristotle more carefully,' replied Alexander calmly. 'They are elephants.' Three years had passed since Alexander had crossed the Hellespont and he was now twenty-five. They were standing on a ridge at a place called Gaugamela to the north of the Persian Empire, looking down on Darius' new army lined up on the dusty plain below. 'At least a million men,' he continued thoughtfully. 'With our new troops from Greece and Macedonia we have 45,000.

And the battlefield has been prepared against us.'

Not only had Darius gathered hundreds of thousands of men from across his empire, he had swept the battlefield clear so that his scythed chariots with sharp blades on their wheels could cut through the Macedonian troops. Spikes and chains had been hammered into the ground to stop Alexander's horses.

'The men are frightened, Alexander,' said old Parmenion. 'This will be an impossible battle.'

'No,' replied Alexander with a smile. 'It is lucky for us. Darius has brought all the men he has. After we win this battle, Persia will have nothing left to stop us.'

'But how can we win against so many?'

'Tell the men to get some sleep, I will give you my battle plan in the morning,' replied the king.

Alexander stayed up late that night, watching 100,000 fires glowing like a carpet of flames in the dark where the vast Persian army was camped, drawing up his plans. Then he went to bed and slept as if there was nothing in the world to worry about.

Next morning, the Macedonian king woke late

and rode among his fearful troops, giving his orders cheerfully and calling out encouragement. Above, Alexander spotted an eagle – the symbol of Zeus – flying straight towards the enemy.

'You see,' he shouted, pointing to the sky. 'Zeus himself leads us into battle, and if I am truly his son, then the gods will bring us victory.'

Every man in the army took courage from Alexander. They, too, were starting to believe that their leader was the son of Zeus, a hero who would never be beaten. And now here was a sign that the gods were with him. Soon they were marching forward to meet the Persians. As always, Alexander rode fearlessly in front, this time dressed in flashing, glittering armour studded with jewels.

As the two armies clashed, Darius' scythed chariots thundered down on the left flank of the army, the deadly blades on the wheels whirring. But Alexander had expected this. First archers and javelin throwers moved forward. As spears and arrows thudded among the chariots, screaming horses went down, tangling the chariots behind. Still, the chariots that remained charged on.

Following Alexander's orders, his men did

something the Persians had never seen before. Great holes opened in the Macedonian line of men. The Persian charioteers stared in disbelief as their enemy simply got out of the way. Through another hail of arrows and spears, the chariots raced straight past and found themselves behind Alexander's army, where they should have been able to attack from the rear. But before the chariots could turn, a great mass of serving boys, grooms and young squires, who never usually fought in battle, fell upon them. Darius' chariots were no more.

At the front, Alexander had no time to enjoy the Persian wails of fear as their deadly chariots were destroyed. The Macedonian horses swept around for an attack and charged through clouds of dust screaming 'Alalalalalai'. The foot soldiers had pulled the fighting away from the war elephants and the traps that Darius had set, and now Alexander could launch a cavalry attack on the Persians where it would matter most: at Darius himself.

Deep within the troops, Darius looked on in shock as Alexander's horsemen roared into his colossal, unbeatable army, cutting down any man who got in their way. The Persians were no match for the Macedonians' skill and ferocity.

Darius saw Alexander in shining armour riding a great, black, snorting horse with a white blaze on its brow. As the horse lashed out with its hooves, Alexander drew back his arm and hurled a spear. It missed Darius, but brought down the man next to him. Shaking with terror, the Great King of the Persians turned his chariot and fled for his life. Calling for his men to follow him, Alexander began slashing his way through Persian troops to give chase.

Once again, Darius escaped. Behind Alexander and his men, the battle still raged and Parmenion's troops were in danger of being overwhelmed. With a shout of frustration, Alexander pulled on Bucephalus' reins and led the cavalry back into the fight. It didn't last long. With the Great King gone, the heart had gone out of the Persians and they scattered, some following Darius, but most disappearing to return to their homes. The battlefield was littered with the Persian dead.

Covered in dust, sweat and blood, Hephaestion turned to Alexander. 'You are truly the King of

Persia now!' he shouted.

'Not until Darius kneels before me,' came Alexander's angry reply.

13

Persia Falls

From Gaugamela, Alexander marched south to the legendary city of Babylon. News of his victory had already reached the city and the gates were opened to him as if he were already the Great King. Flowers were thrown in his path and people lined the streets to welcome the conqueror. As he passed through the shouting crowds, Alexander stared in wonder at Babylon's stepped temple with its famous gardens planted high above the city, and the vast royal palaces, each of which had hundreds of rooms and contained enough treasure to make Alexander the richest man in the world.

For a few weeks, Alexander rested in Babylon, enjoying his new city, showering his men with gold and silver, and allowing them to enjoy all the delights the place had to offer. But the urge to follow Darius and see the rest of Persia was too strong for Alexander to stay for long. Soon, his army was marching again, first to the Persian capital of Susa, which opened its gates without a fight, too. In the Great King's palace, Alexander found even more gold, as well as statues from the Greek city of Athens, which had been stolen during a Persian attack many years before. Alexander ordered them to be sent back to their true home.

Next, he marched north to Persepolis, where the Great Kings were crowned on a golden throne within yet another fabulous palace. At last, the Macedonian king sat on the throne of Persia, but Alexander was still not satisfied. He knew that while Darius was still free, he could never be the true ruler.

Up until now, he had always treated any city that surrendered to him fairly, but in Persepolis Alexander's anger was roused. Surrounded by old carvings that told the story of how the Persians had once burned Athens to the ground, he decided to show that he, too, could be ruthless. Taking the enormous fortune of gold and silver for himself, Alexander allowed his army to strip whatever they could from the mighty palace, and then ordered it to be set ablaze.

With the wreckage of the Great King's most important residence still smoking behind him, Alexander set off to find Darius himself. His spies told him that he had gone north into the mountains and Alexander was determined to find him, so that the Great King would know that he'd been beaten once and for all. After that, Alexander had already decided to treat Darius kindly. He would be returned to his family and allowed to live quietly somewhere where he couldn't cause trouble.

For weeks, Alexander and his men marched up the rough mountain road that Darius and the remains of his army had taken. Away from Persepolis, and with his enemy not far ahead, Alexander's mood brightened. Seeing an old soldier struggling along with a heavy bundle on his back, the king stopped him and asked, 'What are you carrying that's so heavy?'

'It's gold from your treasury, sire,' the soldier replied with a grunt. 'You have so much of it now.'

The king grinned. 'Not quite so much any more,' he replied. 'Whatever you're carrying, you can keep. That should make it easier to bear!'

Alexander rode off laughing, leaving the man speechless. On his back was a fortune large enough to keep him like a king for the rest of his days.

Weeks passed with no sight of Darius' army. Then, suddenly, scouts saw a few tired Persians on the road. They told Alexander that Darius had been arrested by his own commanders and put in chains. Quickly, the king ordered a group of horsemen to follow him and set off along the road at a gallop.

Two days later, the small party came across the remains of a camp. Wagons stood empty, but no sign of Darius could be found. Glumly, Alexander told his men to rest. One walked down to a nearby stream to fetch drinking water and found another wagon on its side, covered in mud.

'Come quickly, Alexander,' he shouted a few moments later, running into the camp.

The king followed him and peered into the abandoned wagon. Inside, wrapped in chains made of gold, was the Great King of Persia, Darius III.

He had been stabbed to death.

Alexander was furious. Although Darius was his enemy, he had been a king. Gently, Alexander took his own cloak and covered the body with it, then gave orders that Darius was to be taken to Persepolis for a full royal funeral.

A few days later, Alexander sat in his tent with his chin in his hands, thinking. With Darius dead, he felt, at last, that he was the true King of Persia, yet he was not as happy as he should have been. He could not allow Darius' murder to go unpunished and the remains of the Persian army were dangerous, too. And deep within his heart, the spirit of adventure was pulling Alexander further east, to see for himself all the wonders of which Aristotle had spoken.

Lost in thought, he was irritated when he heard a commotion outside the tent. A richly dressed Persian noble was approaching through the forest, followed by a boy of about sixteen.

Alexander came out of his tent, frowning, as the man came forward and bowed. 'I have come to plead for my life,' he said. 'I was among those who arrested Darius, although I did not kill him.

If you allow me to go my own way, I will tell you what happened to the Great King and, if you will have him, I will give you Darius' own favourite servant.' The man pointed to the boy.

Alexander looked him up and down. He was the most handsome young man the king had ever seen, with deep brown eyes and shining black hair that fell to his shoulders.

'And what do you want, boy?' Alexander asked gruffly. 'I won't have any servant who does not follow me freely.'

The boy fell to his knees and looked up at Alexander with awe. 'It would be an honour to serve Your Majesty,' he whispered.

'His name is Bagoas,' said the noble man.

'I accept your offer,' said Alexander. 'Now tell me about those who killed Darius.'

'The leader is a general called Bessus. He argued that Darius had led Persia from defeat to disaster, which is true, and then he killed him. Bessus tells his followers that he is now the Great King.'

'Then I will follow this Bessus and he will answer to a true king,' spat Alexander.

14

A Plot Uncovered

Alexander clapped Parmenion on the shoulder. 'Our ways must part for a while at least, old friend,' he told the general. 'I will take half the men into the mountains of Bactria, to hunt Bessus, but I need to leave the other half behind to guard the treasure and in case of trouble in Persia.'

Parmenion nodded. He would never have admitted it, but he was grateful that he would not have to make the difficult mountain journey. He was over seventy years old now, and starting to feel weary.

Alexander had noticed that Parmenion was not as tough as he used to be and had chosen this task for him specially. It was an important job, and one that showed how much trust Alexander placed in him, but it would allow Parmenion to rest in the warm town of Hamadan. From there, the old general could make sure that crucial messages reached Alexander in the mountains, while being able to march back towards the main Persian cities should the need arise.

'I'll leave you with 20,000 men,' Alexander continued. 'But I'll take Philotas. I would feel lost without at least one of your family close by.'

'Thank you, Alexander. I am sure my son will serve you better than I could at my age.'

Alexander laughed. 'Don't think I'm finished with you yet, old man. You've plenty of battles left in you.'

With 30,000 men, Alexander went south and east across the Seistan Desert towards the steep and dangerous Hindu Kush mountains, where Bessus was hiding and building a new army. For a month, he marched across the barren plain, a fierce wind continually blowing dust in the face of every man.

A halt was called one evening near the town of Farah and, as the tents were put up, Bagoas

LIVESinACTION

saw Alexander looking dusty and tired. With a few words, the Persian boy ordered a warm bath to be made ready so that, when he entered the tent, Alexander was surprised and grateful. Still thanking Bagoas, he undressed and sank into the warm water with a sigh. Then he closed his eyes, and listened to the wind howling outside.

Alexander's eyes opened suddenly when a young man called Cebalinus pushed his way into the tent, and dropped to his knees before Alexander's bath, sweating and trembling.

'Is there trouble?' Alexander demanded, half rising from the warm water.

'A plot, sire. There is a plot to kill you and replace you with a new king,' the boy stammered.

'Bagoas!' Alexander shouted.

The dark Persian boy had overheard everything and had already signalled for guards, who took hold of Cebalinus roughly while Alexander scrambled from the bath and into his clothes.

'Who is behind this plot and how long have you known about it?' Alexander demanded of the shaking Cebalinus.

'My brother told me about it two days ago.

86

He heard from a friend of his called Dimnus.'

'Two *days*! You have kept this a secret for two whole days?' demanded Alexander, white with fury.

'No, *no*!' screamed Cebalinus, as the guard forced his arm up his back, almost breaking it. 'I told Philotas. He said he would pass the message on to you.'

Alexander made a signal, and the guard dropped Cebalinus, panting, to the ground. 'Take him and keep him safe,' the king hissed. 'And bring me this Dimnus.'

An hour later, Bagoas squatted quietly in a corner and listened as Alexander spoke with his friends. Warned by the shouts coming from Alexander's tent, Dimnus had killed himself to avoid the king's fury, but the matter had not ended there.

'I cannot believe Philotas knew of this for two days and said nothing,' whispered Ptolemy in disbelief.

'There can be no reason for it, unless –' began Hephaestion.

'Unless he was involved in the plot,' finished Alexander grimly. 'Have the guards arrest him and search his tent. He will stand trial in the morning.'

Ptolemy was thoughtful for a moment. 'And if he is guilty, then what about Parmenion?' he said at last. 'Even if the old man is not involved, he is behind us with 20,000 men and all the treasure of Persia. If he finds out that his son has been put to death for plotting to kill the king, who knows what he may do.'

'I've already thought of that,' said Alexander. 'It's a dangerous situation. Philotas is the only son Parmenion has and if he chose to lead his men against us, we would have to fight him. The whole army might be destroyed.'

The following morning, Philotas was brought before the silent army in chains. The law said that his crime should by tried by the men of Macedonia and Alexander was determined that Philotas would face justice by the rules of his home country. Alexander stood before the gathered men with the desert wind whipping sun-streaked hair around his face and shouted out the charge – Philotas was involved in a plot to kill him.

Philotas shouted that he was innocent, but Alexander's men had been busy during the night. Seven other men were bought forward. Every one of them admitted they had been part of the plot, and Philotas was their leader.

Alexander turned his head as the men of Macedonia declared that Philotas and the seven others were guilty. There could only be one punishment and, as Alexander walked away, the Macedonian army made sure that Philotas would never plot against the king again.

Almost as soon as Philotas was dead, a racing camel galloped from the camp at Farah toward Hamadan. It carried a letter for Parmenion and another for his second-in-command.

Almost without stopping, the camel ran across the desert at a speed no horse could have matched and a few days later, old Parmenion opened his message from Alexander.

'He reports that all is well, and sends me greetings from my son,' Parmenion called to the soldier by his side, who had also opened a letter from Alexander.

Carefully, the second-in-command read his instructions from the king again. Then he drew his sword and killed the old general as Alexander had ordered.

15

Darker Days

A year later, in 329 BC, Alexander stared grimly at the man who stood before him, his hands tied and with his head in a wooden collar.

For twelve long months, Alexander and his army had chased Bessus into Bactria, the wild mountain country far to the north-east of the Persian Empire. Sometimes the army had almost starved, sometimes they had been forced to crawl through raging storms of snow and ice as they crossed the terrible Hindu Kush. Now, like Darius before him, Bessus had been betrayed by his own men. They had been terrified by the lengths that Alexander was prepared to go to catch them and knew that the king would never allow them to surrender.

To save themselves, they had given Bessus to Alexander for punishment.

'Why did you kill your lawful king?' Alexander gently asked the shaking man.

'It was the others, not me... I wanted to spare Darius, but they forced me to kill him,' stuttered Bessus.

'But then you declared yourself the Great King,' replied Alexander.

'I had to...'

'Enough,' ordered Alexander sharply. 'You are a liar, a traitor and a murderer and you will be punished for your crimes.'

Bessus was led away to prison. Within weeks, he would be dead. Alexander had learned the lessons of kingship well and could not allow such a dangerous man to live.

Alexander had changed over a hard year of marching. Now, he wore the jewelled circlet of the Persian king around his head, and his dress had changed, too. Although no Macedonian would ever stoop to wearing trousers like the Persians, he often wore the Persian royal tunic of striped white and purple. From Bagoas, he was also learning a few words of Persian as well as the ways of the Persian kings, who were treated like gods on earth. The handsome Persian boy had become a close friend, as well as Alexander's servant. Now, he rarely left the king's side.

Although Alexander was careful that his own men never had to bow before him like the Persians he conquered, there were mutterings that the king had gone too far and was becoming no better than a Persian himself. Alexander thought about this long and hard. He hated upsetting the men who had followed him so far from their homes, but he knew that to rule his new empire well he had to understand the Persian ways. Just as the Macedonians would not accept anyone but a Macedonian king, the Persians expected a ruler who acted like a Persian Great King.

With Bessus defeated and his rebellion scattered, there was nothing to stop Alexander from returning to take his throne in any one of his Persian cities, or even in Pella. Alexander had achieved the impossible – all the wealth and the throne of Persia were now his. He was a king and a god in Egypt, and King of Macedonia, too. Alexander had arrived in Persia just five years ago and he was now twenty-seven. Only the furthest and most rugged stretch of the Persian Empire remained unconquered, and beyond that was India. Alexander could easily have turned his back on the wild mountain lands and returned to a life of luxury, but though his friends sometimes suggested it, Alexander's sense of adventure pulled him onwards.

'What would I do if I went back?' he asked them. 'Grow old sitting on a throne signing papers? Where is the glory in that?'

And so Alexander marched his men slowly east, and then south toward the mysterious land of India.

In the wilds of the Persian north-west frontier, the tribes were as rebellious as those of Thrace. Every step of the way, Alexander was forced to fight and often burn whole villages as a sign of what those who did not accept him as king could expect. Often, he made peace with a tribe, only for them to rebel again as soon as he had left. When that happened, he was forced to turn around and fight again.

Finally, he stopped the army to rest in the

mountain city of Samarkand. Tired of fighting, recovering from a wound he had received in battle, and in need of some fun to lighten his mood, the king invited his friends and commanders to join him for some food and wine.

Among Alexander's guests was a man known as Cleitus the Black, who was the brother of Alexander's childhood nurse Lanike. He had also once saved Alexander's life in battle on the River Granicus. As the evening passed, Cleitus swigged wine. Alexander, too, drank more than usual. As the two men swallowed cup after cup, they began to argue and soon it turned into a bitter quarrel. All the men were weary and homesick after a long year of fighting and terrible hardship, and tempers were easily lost. Cleitus was also upset that Alexander was about to send him to govern one of the new cities he had ordered to be built in the mountains. Cleitus knew Alexander thought he was a bad commander and wanted him out of the way, and it meant that Cleitus would have to stay in a land that he hated for many years to come.

When insults began to fly, Alexander's friends led the drunk Cleitus away and threw him out of the tent. But moments later he staggered back in, roaring, 'You might be Great King of Persia, but you'll never be as great as your father!'

'My father could never have conquered all that I have done,' Alexander shouted back, his face red.

'But Philip was a proper Macedonian warrior who didn't wear pretty crowns, keep a Persian boy as a pet, and dress like a barbarian,' spat Cleitus.

It was a deadly insult. Alexander grabbed a spear from a guard close by and ran Cleitus through with it. As the man who had once saved his life died on the floor, Alexander sank to his knees with his head in his hands.

'What have I done?' he wept. 'I have killed my friend.'

For three days these were the only words Alexander spoke. He did not move from his bed or eat or drink. Only Bagoas and Hephaestion were allowed to come near him, and both tried their best to talk their king round.

'He was a drunken fool and deserved to die for daring to quarrel with you,' whispered Bagoas.

'The men are all on your side,' Hephaestion told him. 'They say that Cleitus was a difficult man and a bad soldier who will not be missed, and that you did the right thing by killing him.'

Finally, Alexander allowed them to bring him food and clothes, but it would be months before he smiled again.

16

Love and Peace

With Alexander still sunk in gloom over the death of Cleitus, the army continued to march, only stopping to defeat any villages or towns that refused to accept the Macedonian as their king.

At last, in 327 BC, the troops came to a stronghold that was perched on a rocky crag called Koh-i-nor. The town on its peak looked impossible to capture. It was protected by a deep ravine so that there was nowhere for Alexander's army to attack the town walls. Great siege engines were built to toss stones and arrows into the enemy fort and, seeing that Alexander would not stop until his town was reduced to rubble, the ruler – a man named Oxyartes – surrendered.

Alexander always treated those who gave in to him with friendship and rode into the city to make peace with Oxyartes, who had hastily arranged a banquet. During the feast, Alexander happened to look up. Across the room was the most beautiful woman he had ever seen. With shining black eyes, she gazed back at him, then smiled.

'Who is that?' Alexander whispered.

'My daughter, Roxane,' Oxyartes replied proudly. 'Her name means "Little Star" and she is said to be the loveliest woman in all the Persian Empire.'

Alexander agreed; he had fallen in love at first sight. But he had no time to stay at Koh-i-nor and get to know Roxane. That night, he told Hephaestion, 'I shall ask her father for her hand in marriage tomorrow.'

'But you have only seen her once,' Hephaestion protested. 'And you are Great King of Persia, the most powerful man in the world. You should marry an important woman, not some unknown girl from a small fort in the middle of nowhere.'

Aleaxander grinned. He was in love and, for the first time in months, his grief over the death of Cleitus was forgotten. 'What is the point of being the most powerful man in the world if I can't do exactly as I please?' he asked.

Oxyartes was delighted to allow his daughter to marry the Great King and Alexander quickly arranged a wedding ceremony as lavish as could be organised by an army on the march. For days the small town on its rocky crag was filled with the sound of musicians and singers. Great feasts were prepared and generous gifts given to the army and to Oxyartes. And when Alexander first kissed his new bride, he knew that he had made the right decision.

All too soon it was time to move on again. Alexander was eager to reach India. He could not bear to be parted from Roxane, though, and it was quickly decided that she would travel with him. For once, Alexander was nervous.

'Perhaps you should wait here for me after all, my love,' he whispered to her the night before the army was due to march. 'The road ahead might be dangerous. We are going into a strange land and no one knows what lies in wait there. There will be more fighting and –'

Roxane stopped him with a kiss, then asked

quietly, 'But if I am not safe by the side of the greatest hero in the world, where *will* I be safe?'

The next morning, with the usual clatter of armour, horses whinnying, and men complaining as they shouldered their loads, the army set off once again. The journey ahead was not as difficult as the roads behind them, but Alexander was determined to travel slowly. For years his men had followed him through danger and hardship and were battle-weary and ragged, but now summer was coming. The weather was pleasantly warm in the mountains, without the scorching heat of the low country, and Alexander allowed his army to enjoy the clear sunshine, marching at a restful pace.

Throughout the early summer, he was forced to lead his forces back to forts and strongholds already conquered to put down more uprisings, but as the weeks passed, the rebellions ended. Now, Alexander and his army were able to enjoy a rare time of peace and plenty. The army stopped often to hunt birds and animals. They ate well and Alexander organised games and wrestling matches in camp to keep his men entertained. With Roxane always close by, Alexander forgot about Darius and Bessus and Cleitus and all the cares of conquering an empire. Instead, he laughed and joked with his friends as if they were boys again and back at Mieza.

As the summer drew to an end, Alexander gazed down from the foothills of the Hindu Kush at the plains of a vast new land – India. His heart was beating like a war drum. Here, at last, was the mysterious place that few had ever visited, a whole new country waiting to be conquered. It was said that beyond India was the end of the world itself and what greater glory could there be than winning an empire that stretched to the very ends of the Earth? Patting Bucephalus on the neck, Alexander gave the order for his men to march.

17
Into India

After the restful summer, in 327 BC, Alexander prepared for war again. India would be his greatest prize and he was determined to win it. But ten years of fighting had taught him to be careful. First, he needed to make sure that he left behind no unconquered people who might attack his army from the rear.

Alexander gave his orders. Hephaestion was to go south and build a bridge over the River Indus so that when Alexander arrived, the army could cross the water easily. Luckily, Hephaestion had a guide to show him the way; a friendly Indian king, or *rajah* as he called himself, who had seen Alexander's army and quickly surrendered. Alexander would go east, conquering the tribes that lived in the foothills of the mountains.

As always, Alexander had chosen the most difficult, and exciting, task. The forts and towns of the foothills were difficult to reach and even more difficult to attack. They were often protected by steep cliffs and winter was coming, which made the march more difficult. Nevertheless, as the skies grew dimmer and snow began to fall, Alexander continued to lead his men east. Fortress after fortress fell to him, though the fighting was fierce. During one battle, he was hit in the ankle by an arrow, but still the king fought on until his army had pushed its enemies back to a giant, flat-topped rock known as Pir-Sar.

Astride Bucephalus, Alexander peered up at the heights of Pir-Sar. Never had he seen a place so difficult to assault. It made Koh-i-nor look like a child's toy.

Panting, his old friend Eumenes came riding to his side. 'It cannot be done, Alexander,' he said seriously. 'I took a party and rode around it.' The cliffs must be a mile high at least and I wouldn't ask a mountaineer to climb them, let alone an army. Herakles himself could not have conquered this place.'

Alexander turned to look at Eumenes. 'Even more reason for me to do so,' he said simply.

The next day, Alexander found what he was looking for. To the north was a smaller rock that almost joined Pir-Sar. Its cliffs were easier to ascend and, at the top, Alexander's troops would be hidden by trees. Taking a few friends, Alexander climbed up then signalled for the army to follow. It took two days for every man to reach the top and still the most difficult task lay ahead of them. Between Alexander's army and Pir-Sar was a ravine as wide as a river and hundreds of feet deep.

'What now?' asked Eumenes, looking into the depths of the ravine in despair. Alexander just smiled, and said, 'Remember Mount Ossa?' as he kicked a rock into the giant gorge.

For a day, twenty-five thousand men cut down trees to build a bridge and pushed rocks and soil into the great ravine. At first, the warriors of Pir-Sar laughed at the attempt to cross empty air, but little by little, inch by inch, the army achieved the impossible once again – a jutting bridge that stretched halfway across the ravine. With their laughter turned to unbelieving horror, the defenders of Pir-Sar watched as Alexander's great siege engines were rolled forward.

Rocks and arrows were hurled across while Alexander ordered his men to climb the walls of the ravine and attack. Great rewards were promised to the first man to the top. Many dropped to their deaths as the defenders threw boulders down at them, but still they tried.

On the night of the third day, Alexander could wait no longer and went down into the ravine himself. Grunting with effort, he began the long climb to the top of Pir-Sar and arrived in time to watch the tribesmen fleeing. With hundreds of men now climbing up to join him, Alexander launched an attack. The last enemy that stood between him and India was quickly defeated.

Impatient to see the mysterious new land, Alexander led his army to the bridge across the River Indus that Hephaestion had finished building months ago. Once across, the Macedonians gazed in wonder at the Indian men they passed along the road; they wore earrings made from the ivory tusks of elephants and dyed their beards every shade of the rainbow.

For a few days, Alexander rested his army at the mud-brick city of Taxila. Ambhi, the friendly *rajah* who had already helped Hephaestion, lavished gifts upon him, including thirty war elephants and 5,000 men. Alexander was delighted and, in return, showered Ambhi with gold from Persia. Most importantly, Ambhi also had news of what Alexander would soon face.

'The lands to the south are flat, an easy march for your men that will take a week or so,' Ambhi told him. 'But after that you will come to the River Jhelum and beyond that are the lands of a *rajah* named Porus. He has a great army and many elephants trained for war. If he decides to give battle, it will not be easy for you to defeat him.'

This was not good news. The strength of Alexander's army was the cavalry horses, and the horses were terrified of the great elephants. Nevertheless, he ordered the men to march once again and sent messengers ahead to Porus with demands that he meet Alexander to surrender. Soon, Porus sent his own message back. He would meet Alexander, but only on the battlefield. There would be no surrender.

Porus was as good as his word. As Alexander approached the River Jhelum, he could see a great army lined up on the opposite bank. Rising among the mass of men, like small fortresses, were three hundred elephants, each of which had archers and spearmen riding on its back. When they saw the army on the other side of the river, the elephants lifted their trunks and trumpeted loudly, making the Macedonian horses whinny with fear. Like Alexander's first battle in Persia, at the River Granicus, the stretch of water between his army and Porus' would make it impossible to attack without having thousands of men killed while they struggled across. Once again, Alexander would have to be cunning.

'Take scouts up and down the river,' he told Hephaestion, 'and find me a crossing place.' To Ptolemy he said, 'Prepare great stores of food where Porus can see them. I want him to think that we will wait here for a long time.'

As the two men turned to carry out their orders, Alexander called them back. 'Wait, I'm not finished,' he said. 'I also want men riding in parties at all times of the day and soldiers lined up as if to attack at any minute. I want Porus to be so confused that he cannot guess what we might do.'

For two weeks, Alexander's army did exactly what the king ordered. One moment, they dug trenches and built huts as if they might wait for months, the next, men were lined up on the banks of the River Jhelum as if they might attack at any moment. In the middle of the night, Alexander's cavalry thundered out of camp shouting 'Alalalalalai', forcing Porus to rouse his men from their beds and prepare for an attack that never came.

Meanwhile, Hephaestion had returned to the camp with news. 'There is a place about seventeen miles upriver where we might cross,' he told Alexander. It is hidden by trees, and though the water is deep, the horses should be able to swim across and we can easily make some boats.'

Alexander clapped him on the shoulder with a grin.

A few nights later, the king led 5,000 cavalry and 11,000 foot soldiers away from camp. To Porus it looked like just another trick. But this time, it wasn't. Seventeen miles upriver, Alexander looked out across the water. 'You were right, Hephaestion,' he said. 'It's a difficult crossing, but not impossible. Let's get started.'

At that moment, it began to rain. Within moments, heavy drops were pouring from the sky in great sheets that soaked Alexander's men and made the ground slippery with thick mud. 'Quickly!' shouted Alexander. 'Before the river begins to flood.'

With rain lashing down on them, men and horses took to the river, to slip and slide up the opposite bank covered in mud. There, they were spotted by one of Porus' scouts, who immediately raced off to warn his own army.

'It doesn't matter,' shouted Alexander grimly. 'Keep going!'

Within two hours, Porus had sent a force out to meet Alexander, but the *rajah* was about to find out why the Macedonian horsemen were the best in the world. Like Darius, he sent his chariots forward to give battle, but they became stuck in the thick mud as Alexander led his cavalry against them in tight formation. Javelins and arrows flew through the dark night and drenching rain. Before long, Porus' chariots were utterly defeated.

'Halt!' shouted Alexander, with his fist held to the sky. 'Foot soldiers forward.'

The trembling, sweaty and filthy horses of the cavalry stopped. Now, Alexander's stony-faced infantry marched to the front.

Porus sent his own men and elephants to meet them. Alexander gave another signal and urged Bucephalus on. In rain and darkness, the cavalry swept forward once more, keeping away from the elephants that the horses hated, but throwing arrows and spears into the Indian army, as they screamed 'Alalalalai'.

Porus' archers shot back. Alexander gasped when an arrow flew out of the night and thudded into the horse beneath him. Bucephalus screamed and staggered, as Alexander threw his arms around the horse's great neck to stop himself from being thrown off.

As Alexander's beloved horse died, the battle continued. The foot soldiers swarmed among the elephants chopping at them with axes and swords while the men that Alexander had left in camp swept across the river at last. Caught between them, and with his panicking elephants trampling their own army, Porus watched as his men were cut to pieces.

Kneeling in the mud in the midst of the fighting, Alexander held the great head of Bucephalus in his lap and sobbed. They had fought their last battle together.

18
Alexander Defeated

Alexander could not believe what he was hearing. His army had followed him across 11,500 miles to the north of India. Everywhere they had been, they had found glory. They had fought against vast Persian armies and fierce hill tribes. Cities that had been thought impossible to conquer had fallen before them and new cities had been built.

It was 326 BC, just three months after Alexander had scored his great victory against Porus, and the army had been marching ever since. Now across the River Beas, the whole of India lay before them. Alexander tilted his head to one side in the pouring rain and made a signal for Coenus to continue.

The grizzled old soldier looked Alexander in

the eye and said roughly, 'Your men are tired, Alexander. They have followed you across the world. Look at them. Their clothes are in rags and their boots are leaking. For three months it hasn't stopped raining. As soon as we clean our weapons, they begin to rust again. It is time to go back and enjoy the fruits of our victories.'

Alexander was horrified. He had only just begun to conquer India. To the south he had been told there was another vast empire waiting to be toppled. An empire that no one in Greece had even known existed. It was old and rich and weak and Alexander was determined to be the man who had conquered two empires.

'If you will not follow me, I'll go on by myself,' he hissed. 'You can go back to Macedonia and tell them that you left your king to fight alone.'

Coenus looked at Alexander sadly. The Macedonian men still loved their leader despite the hardships they had been forced to endure, but they were tired, wet, hungry and footsore and had already achieved more than any army in history. What else, they asked themselves, could Alexander expect of them?

Slowly, Coenus shook his head.

Alexander stayed in his tent for two days, speaking to no one but his closest friends. It was a bitter disappointment, but he couldn't go on without the Macedonian army behind him. The greatest march in history had come to an end. Eventually, he sighed and looked up at Hephaestion. 'After all the battles we have won together, I am finally defeated by my own army,' he said wearily.

Hephaestion laid a hand on his friend's shoulder. 'You know that I would have followed you anywhere,' he said softly.

Alexander nodded, then left the tent to speak to his men.

'Very well, we will go back,' he shouted to the cheering army. 'But first we will build here twelve giant altars to each of the gods, to honour them and mark how far we have come. Then the army will split in two. Ten thousand men will return the way we came. The rest will return with me by a new route.'

As the cheering continued, Alexander finally allowed himself a small and bitter smile. Even though he had been forced to go back, it would not stop him from seeing new lands, and adding them to his empire.

In eight years, Alexander had conquered the Persian Empire, which had been thought an impossible task. And more. He had travelled thousands of miles, fighting every step of the way, and not once had his army been beaten in battle. He had explored lands that few had ever seen. He had spoken with the gods and been worshipped as a god himself. He had more riches than anyone in history. Alexander's goal had been to prove himself the equal of the legendary hero Achilles, and now no one could doubt that he was even mightier. Already men had begun calling him by a new name.

Shaking his head in sadness, Alexander the Great turned back towards his tent where Roxane was waiting for him.

Epilogue
The End of The March

Alexander's decision to find a new way back to his Persian lands was to prove a fatal mistake. Always the adventurer, he was determined to find a way to travel between India and Persia by river and sea, so that in future men would not have to make the long and dangerous journey across the mountains. During the journey, disaster after disaster struck and he was almost killed several times.

Alexander ordered eight hundred boats to be built to carry men, horses and supplies downstream to the sea. Almost all of them were smashed to pieces on the river rocks within days of their setting out. Alexander himself was forced to swim for his life.

The tribes and cities they passed fought fiercely, too, and Alexander's men were unwilling to risk their lives any more. During one battle, Alexander jumped alone from a high wall into a town of warriors and was only just saved after being hit in the chest by an arrow. The wound nearly killed him, but within a week he was on his feet again.

The greatest danger came during the final part of the journey. One last test remained to Alexander's army – crossing the Makran Desert. It was a vast and lonely place of great dunes. Alexander knew it would be difficult to do, but the ordeal was to prove much, much harder than he expected.

In the end, it took sixty days and Alexander's men died by the thousand. The sun was so fierce they could only move by night, when their exhausted legs had to carry them up countless steep sand dunes, sinking to the knee at every step. Food soon ran out and the starving men were forced to eat their own horses. The few plants the army found were poisonous, and deadly snakes struck many more down. Alexander began the journey with 40,000 men. He arrived at the edge of Persia, on the other side of the desert, with less than 15,000.

For the rest of his life, Alexander was haunted by memories of the Makran Desert, and he often wept over the 25,000 brave men who had been left in the sand. To make matters worse, as he neared the centre of his empire at last, he found that many of the men he had left behind to guard his lands had rebelled or stolen from him. Few had expected him to return alive from his distant travels. Alexander's great Persian Empire was crumbling.

With the fury of a man who had seen brave and loyal men die while those who'd stayed behind in safety had betrayed him, Alexander took his revenge. As he marched towards Susa in the spring of 324 BC, he left behind a trail of hanged victims. Everyone was to know that the Great King had returned and that the punishment for those who had wronged him would be harsh.

When Persia was secure once more, Alexander became determined to put the past behind him and enjoy the wealth and glory his adventures had brought. He had more money than anyone in the world had ever possessed and began to spend it on a grand scale. First, the king arranged an enormous wedding ceremony that would show the world that the kingdom of Macedonia and the empire of Persia would become one. During days of celebrations, ninety noble Persian women were married to Alexander's friends and commanders. There were games and feasts and theatre, and every new couple received generous presents from their king.

When the 10,000 men arrived from India, Alexander marched a part of the way back towards Macedonia with them and gave a huge feast in their honour. Every man was presented with a reward; enough money to last them a lifetime.

Next, Alexander arranged a great carnival of games at the Persian summer palace of Hamadan. Athletes, actors and artists arrived from all over the empire to compete against each other before their glorious king.

He was enjoying the competitions with a cup of wine in his hand when a messenger arrived. Hephaestion, who had been put to bed with a chill, had taken a turn for the worse. The cup dropped from Alexander's grasp. Quickly, he rushed to the bedside of his greatest friend. But by the time he got there, Hephaestion was dead.

Alexander's grief was terrible. For hour upon hour he clung to Hephaestion's body weeping, until finally he was pulled away. For weeks, he could speak to no one.

It was as if Hephaestion's death signalled the final days of Alexander's own life. Although he still made plans for conquests to come, Alexander's energy had faded. In his grief, and still suffering from the chest wound he had taken in India, Alexander the Great became weaker. The young man who had stood looking so healthy and golden before his father at Mieza now spent every night drinking cup after cup of wine and sleeping all day.

As the weeks and months passed, Alexander rarely moved from his palace in Babylon, though on one occasion, soon after Hephaestion's funeral, he took a boat out to explore the city's canals. The waters were famous for causing sickness but, as ever, Alexander refused to think of the danger.

The next night Alexander collapsed on the floor of his bathroom. For ten days he shivered and shook in bed as the world held its breath. Alexander was dying. The Great King, who alone held the mighty empire together, was coming to the end of his life, and no one knew what would happen after.

Unable to speak or move, Alexander raised his hand to salute man after man of his army, who came to his bedside. Finally, with Roxane and Bagoas weeping over his body, the King of Kings passed away. It was June 11, 323 BC, and Alexander was just thirty-two years old. The old high priest of Zeus who had spoken with Queen Olympias before her son was born was finally proved right – the fire that burns the brightest does not burn for long.

Alexander the Great had travelled further and conquered a bigger empire than any man in history. For hundreds of years afterwards, great men would try to recreate his achievements. None truly succeeded. Although greater empires were eventually won, no other leader ever led his men as Alexander had done. None ever crawled through ice alongside their starving army or threw themselves first into the battle. No army would ever again give not only their undying loyalty, but also their love, to a leader as they had done to Alexander the Great.

THRACE

MACEDON

GREECE

Byzantium

Black Sea

Troy *Hellespont*

Gordium

Granicus

CAPPADOCIA

Mieza

Aegean Sea

Miletus

Issus

ARMENIA

Pella

CARIA

CILICIA

Thebes

Athens

CRETE

RHODES

ASSYRI

Mediterranean Sea

CYPRUS

PHOENICIA

Byblos

Sidon

Tyre

SYRIA

BA

Alexandria

Gaza

Ammon Oracle

Memphis

EGYPT

A

LIBYA

River Nile

Red Sea

122

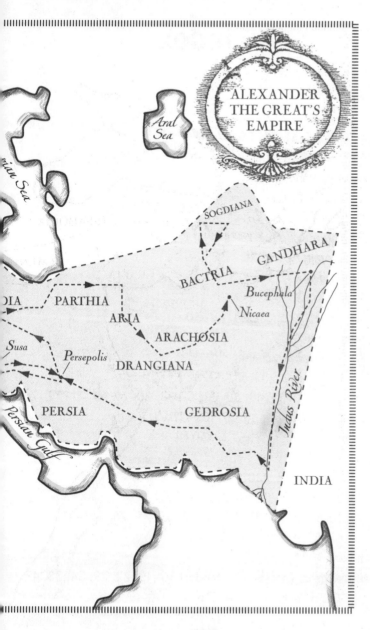

ALEXANDER
THE GREAT'S
EMPIRE

Aral
Sea

...ian Sea

SOGDIANA

GANDHARA

BACTRIA

...DIA   PARTHIA

ARIA

Bucephala

Nicaea

ARACHOSIA

Susa

Persepolis   DRANGIANA

PERSIA   GEDROSIA

Indus River

Persian Gulf

INDIA

123

Index

125

LIVES in ACTION

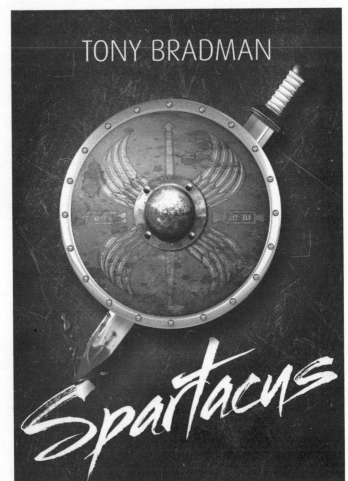

TONY BRADMAN

Spartacus

The story of the rebellious Thracian gladiator